THE WORLD HERITAGE

THE LAND OF THE PHARAOHS

UNESCO

CHILDRENS PRESS®
CHICAGO

Table of Contents

Introduction 4
Ways of Life in Ancient Egypt 6
Religion and the Afterlife 14
Art with a Purpose 18
Timeline of Ancient Egyptian History 22
Memphis: Capital of the Old Kingdom 24
Thebes: Middle and New Kingdoms 26
Nubia and Aswan 30
Glossary 32
Index 33

Library of Congress Cataloging-in-Publication Data

Terzi, Marinella.
  [Imperio de los faraones. English]
  The land of the pharaohs / by Marinella Terzi.
    p.   cm. — (The World heritage)
  Translation of: El imperio de los faraones.
  Includes index.
  Summary: Examines the pyramids, temples, and other existing structures of
ancient Egypt and discusses how they figured in or represent that civilization.
  ISBN 0-516-08378-3
  1. Egypt—Civilization—To 332 B.C.—Juvenile literature. 2. Egypt—Antiquities—
Juvenile literature. [1. Egypt—Civilization—To 332 B.C. 2. Egypt—Antiquities.]
I. Title. II. Series.
DT61.T4318 1992
932'.01—dc20
                                                                    92-7510
                                                                       CIP
                                                                        AC

El Imperio de los Faraones: © INCAFO S.A./Ediciones S.M./UNESCO 1988
The Land of the Pharaohs: © Childrens Press, Inc./UNESCO 1992

ISBN (UNESCO) 92-3-102587-2
ISBN (Childrens Press) 0-516-08378-3

The Land of the Pharaohs

So many tourists visit Egypt, it's hard to imagine the country without them. Busloads of casually dressed sightseers, snapping photos, seem to be everywhere. Over them all stand the silent pyramids, as they have stood for almost five thousand years.

Along the Nile River, from its Delta to the Aswan High Dam, are more than ninety pyramids. There too are temples, sphinxes, and simple tombs called mastabas.

A visitor's eyes meet with centuries of history in the Nile Valley. Naturally, questions arise. How were such enormous monuments built? What was it like to live in ancient Egypt?

Thanks to the work of archaeologists and other scientists, we have some of the answers. Yet many secrets about ancient Egypt remain.

Honoring the Dead

Ancient Egypt is best known for its treatment of the dead. Houses and palaces, villages and towns, have disappeared. But many tombs and their mortuary chapels have survived, despite centuries of tomb-robbing. The top photo shows the pyramid of King Khufu, or Cheops. It is the largest of the three great pyramids at Giza. Below are wall paintings from the tomb of Tut-ankh-Amun ("King Tut") in the Valley of the Kings near Thebes.

4

Ways of Life in Ancient Egypt

From Aswan in the south to the Mediterranean Sea in the north, the Nile River Valley is 560 miles (900 kilometers) long. Along its banks is a fertile strip of land 6 to 9 miles (10 to 15 kilometers) wide. Desert rises on both sides of this rich river valley. Near its mouth, the Nile splits into two main branches. The split forms a triangle-shaped area that the Greeks called the Delta, after a letter of their alphabet.

Most ancient Egyptians lived in the Nile Valley. The first people to settle there arrived about 5500 B.C. Their economy was based mainly on farming. Egyptians grew grains such as barley and emmer wheat. They raised cattle, sheep, goats, and pigs. Every year, farmers looked forward to the flooding of the Nile, for this assured a rich harvest.

In July, monsoons drenched the highlands of East Africa. The rainwater flowed northward into tributaries of the Nile, making the river overflow. As the water flooded the farmers' fields, it deposited a thin layer of rich topsoil.

In November, as the water receded, men and women turned up the soil with simple, wooden plows. They planted grain by stamping it into the ground with their feet. In some areas, they piled up long mounds of earth to trap the rich floodwaters. They also dug canals to bring precious water into the desert. In the warm climate, grain ripened quickly. Most years, people could grow a second crop using irrigation.

Principal Gods and Goddesses

Amun: The invisible god of the air. Represented as a man wearing a headdress with two tall plumes. Introduced as a god of Thebes in Dynasties 11 and 12, Amun became a national god in the New Kingdom period.

Aten: A sun god. Represented by a sun-disk with rays like the spokes of a wheel. The rays end in human hands offering the symbol of life. Akh-en-Aten made him the principal god of Egypt for a short time.

Hat-Hor: Goddess of love and rejoicing. Wife of the god Horus. Sometimes depicted as a cow or as a woman with the head of a cow. Her chief cult center was at Dendera.

Horus: A sky god. Husband of the goddess Hat-Hor. Sometimes represented as a falcon or hawk, or as a man with the head of a falcon. His chief cult center was at Edfu.

Isis: A mother goddess. Sister and wife of Osiris and mother of Horus. She was shown as a woman with the emblem of a throne on her head. Her chief cult center was at Philae.

Osiris: God of the dead, he presided over the underworld. He was represented as a human mummy with kingly robes. His chief cult center was at Abydos.

Ptah: Patron god of artists and craftsmen and one of the gods of creation. He was represented as a man wearing a close-fitting garment and cap. Chief god of the city of Memphis.

Ra: Principal sun god. His chief cult center was at Heliopolis.

Saved from the Waters

About 1300 B.C., the great temple at Abu Simbel was carved out of solid rock. Today, the spot where it stood lies under the waters of Lake Nasser. This artificial lake was formed when the Aswan High Dam was built in the 1960s. At that time, UNESCO took part in a project to save the temple from being covered by the lake. It was cut into blocks and moved to a nearby hill, where it was put back together. The front of the temple is 125 feet (38 meters) high, and the inside is 207 feet (63 meters) deep. The second of the four statues broke off in ancient times. It may have been the result of an earthquake or of a natural crack in the stone. Nearby stands another temple that was saved by modern engineers. The small temple at Abu Simbel, carved from rock, was dedicated to the goddess Hat-Hor and to Queen Nefertari, the wife of Ramesses II.

Besides grain, Egyptians grew melons, beans, lettuce, and onions. They planted date and fig trees. Vineyards in the Nile Delta produced grapes to eat and to make into wine. Egyptians also drank a nourishing, low-alcohol beer made from barley, water, and yeast. There was no sugar. Food was sweetened with honey or fruits such as dates and grapes.

Flax was grown and made into linen cloth, thread, and rope. The papyrus plant, which grew in the marshes of the Delta, was made into a kind of writing paper.

Compared to other ancient lands, Egypt was a rich country. Harvests were usually abundant. When neighboring countries suffered famines, Egypt sometimes sold or gave them grain.

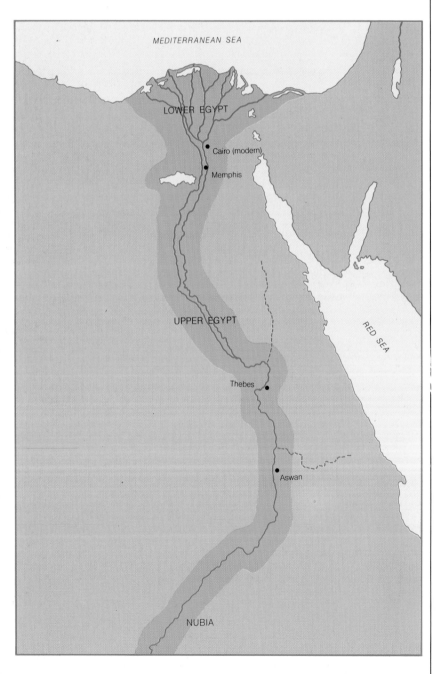

The Power of the Lion

Memphis was the capital of Egypt for much of its long history. The city stood about 15 miles (25 kilometers) from modern Cairo. The photo on the opposite page shows the sphinx in the outdoor archaeological park at the site of ancient Memphis. It was carved from a single block of travertine (Egyptian alabaster). It dates from about 1500-1400 B.C. With the body of a lion and the head of the king, the sphinx represented the king's power. The most famous sphinx in Egypt is the Great Sphinx, guarding the approach to the pyramid of King Kha-ef-Ra at Giza. It is a huge figure, 72 feet (22 meters) high and 243 feet (74 meters) long. The map on the left shows the principal cities of ancient Egypt.

There were three social classes in ancient Egypt. In the upper class were the royal family and other nobility. Most upper-class boys, and a few of the girls, learned to read and write. The small middle class consisted of scribes, artists, craftsmen, professional soldiers, and merchants.

The lowest class, unskilled laborers, was the largest. These were the farmers, ordinary soldiers, and construction workers. Slaves captured in war and criminals had to work in mines and stone quarries. There was little chance for "moving up." Most people spent their whole lives in the same social class. Children nearly always took the same jobs as their parents.

Houses—and even royal palaces—were built of sun-dried mud-bricks. Very few are still standing today. It was not important for homes to last very long. Bricks were cheap and easy to make, so it was easy to repair or replace a home.

The Egyptians believed that their kings were living gods. The king had unlimited power and made all the laws. At the same time, he was expected to do good and to keep order. It was his duty to protect the people from enemies, wild animals, disease, and famine. Kings were praised in times of plenty and blamed in times of want.

Before 3100 B.C., Egypt was divided into two kingdoms: Upper Egypt in the south, and Lower Egypt—the Nile Delta—in the north. Ancient stories tell of a king from the south who united the two kingdoms. His name was Men or Menes, which means "The Founder."

After Egypt was unified, the king sometimes wore a double crown symbolizing the two kingdoms. Many centuries later, one of the titles for Egyptian kings was *per-aa*. This title appears in the Bible in the form "pharaoh."

Houses of Eternity
Thebes was Egypt's capital during the Middle and New Kingdoms. It stood on the west bank of the Nile, opposite the modern town of Luxor. Today on the site of Thebes remains a vast cemetery or necropolis—"city of the dead." It served as the last resting place for the royalty of ancient Thebes. The Valley of the Kings, the Valley of the Queens, and the Tombs of the Nobles are the three principal areas of this necropolis. A tomb was regarded as a person's "House of Eternity." Tombs were furnished with some of the tomb-owner's favorite things. There were also a number of items especially made for use in the after-life. The top photo shows some details from wall paintings in the royal tomb of Pharaoh Ramesses I at Thebes. The photo below shows the great memorial temple of Ramesses III, also in Thebes.

The Kiosk of Qertassi
Though it is small and simple, the Kiosk of Qertassi (*left*) is one of the most precious treasures from ancient Egypt. It was built in the style of Greek and Roman architecture. In 1960, the Egyptian Antiquities Organization moved the charming little temple from its original site in Lower Nubia. Now it stands in the safety of the new outdoor museum near the Aswan High Dam.

Egypt was governed by one dynasty, or ruling family, after another. During the rule of the First Dynasty, Egyptians learned to make papyrus into a kind of paper. Writing became a fine art. Scribes, or professional writers, were highly respected. Instead of an alphabet, ancient Egyptians wrote with characters called hieroglyphs. (See page 22.) The oldest hieroglyphic writings we have found were made in about 3000 B.C.

Egyptians were good at astronomy and mathematics, too. Astronomers set the dates for important religious festivals. They could also predict the date when the Nile would overflow every year. Mathematics was used in designing pyramids, mastabas, and temples.

Egyptians were highly skilled in the science of medicine. Dentists, eye doctors, and internists all served at the royal court. Doctors prescribed cures such as herbs, honey, castor oil, and even animal manure. Prescriptions often included magical spells and prayers to the gods.

Religion and the Afterlife

Religion was important in the Egyptians' daily lives. They saw powerful forces of nature as gods or goddesses. Statues and paintings of the gods showed something about each one's power. Various gods had the form of a falcon, a ram, a lioness, a cow, and so on.

Some gods were worshipped in all of Egypt, such as the sun and the Nile River. The sun god, Ra, was one of the most important gods. Then there was the king himself, considered to be a living god. Each large town had its own special deity, too.

Temples were the houses of the gods and goddesses. Daily rituals took place there. Only purified priests and priestesses could enter the temple's inner rooms. Common people could only enter the first courtyard of the temple, and only on special holidays. Temples were also important commercial centers. They ran schools for scribes, libraries, and medical clinics. They supported the work of artists and craftsmen. Temples owned farm and grazing lands, fleets of ships, mines, slaves, and animals.

Ancient Egyptians may be best known for their belief in life after death. They believed that the afterlife was much like life in this world, only better. And they thought they could take things with them when they died.

14

The Curse of King Tut

On November 4, 1922, a long search was ended. Two Englishmen, archaeologist Howard Carter and his patron Lord Carnarvon, uncovered the lost tomb of Pharaoh Tut-ankh-Amun in the Valley of the Kings. Here was a pharaoh's royal tomb from the fourteenth century B.C., still filled with fabulous treasures!

Tut-ankh-Amun died at a young age, now estimated at 18 to 26. The cause of the young king's death is unknown. He died before a large tomb befitting a pharaoh could be built. Four small chambers of Tut-ankh-Amun's tomb were crammed with thousands of precious objects, many of them made of gold. These treasures are now housed in the Egyptian Museum in Cairo and in the Luxor Museum in Luxor. Tut-ankh-Amun's mummy rests today in a gilt-wood coffin in his tomb in the Valley of the Kings.

Shortly after the discovery of the tomb, Lord Carnarvon died. Newspapers began to spread rumors that he fell victim to an ancient curse for disturbing the peaceful rest of the pharaoh. There is no scientific evidence to support the story. But, to this day, some people believe in the "Curse of Tut-ankh-Amun."

Evolution of the Tombs

Egypt's earliest kings were buried in mastabas. These structures look like pyramids with the top cut off. The king's body was placed in a chamber below the mastaba. Above ground, in the mastaba itself, was a chapel where prayers could be offered for his soul. The first step pyramid was built at Saqqara for King Djoser, of the Third Dynasty. Step pyramids were like several mastabas built on top of each other. Later, true pyramids were given an outer layer of limestone or granite to make their sides smooth.

In upper-class burials, the body was supplied with food, furniture, jewelry, and other beloved objects. Unlike a home for the living, a tomb was built to last. Most of what we know about the ancient Egyptians' way of life has come from studying their tombs.

For the *ka*, or soul, to enter the afterlife, it needed to be enclosed inside something permanent. That is why Egyptians preserved their dead as mummies. However, a statue or painting of the dead person could serve the same purpose.

Turning a body into a mummy is a drying process. Egypt's dry desert climate was ideal for this. A chemical salt called natron was also used to help dry the body. The internal organs were usually removed and dried separately. Egyptians valued the heart as the center of intelligence and feelings. But the brain, thought to be useless, was thrown away.

A proper burial was important, too. At the funeral, a priest performed a ceremony called the Opening of the Mouth. This enabled the *ka* to return to the mummified body.

Some believed that the god Osiris judged a person's earthly life by the Weighing of the Heart. A drawing of this scene appears in ancient papyrus scrolls called the Book of the Dead. The person's heart was weighed on a scale against an ostrich plume, the symbol of truth. Good behavior made the heart light, and sin made it heavy. If the heart and the feather balanced, the soul could pass into eternal life. If the heart sank under the weight of sin, a monster devoured the soul, and the person ceased to exist forever.

The Grandeur of the Temples
The top photo shows the temple of Philae, dedicated to the goddess Isis. It was built during the Ptolemaic Period on an island near Egypt's border with Nubia. Below is a view of the temple of Deir el-Bahri at Thebes. Partially cut out of solid limestone, it was a memorial temple for Queen Hat-shepsut, who ruled Egypt in the 1400s B.C. Ancient Egyptian rulers were usually men. Paintings of Queen Hat-shepsut sometimes show her wearing the clothing of a typical male pharaoh.

A Magical View of the Human Figure
In Egyptian art, part of the human body faces forward and part faces sideways. This can be seen in the reliefs at the left, from the temple of Mandulis at Kalabsha. Nearly all Egyptian art had a magical or religious purpose. In drawing the body, Egyptian artists borrowed an idea from hieroglyphic writing. Each part of the body was treated as a separate "hieroglyph," shown in its most familiar form. The head is shown in profile. The shoulders and upper torso are shown with a front view. The body twists slightly at the waist so that the navel can be shown. Then the legs and feet are shown in profile. The result is an impossibly unnatural pose. But with several different views at the same time, the figure had greater magical value.

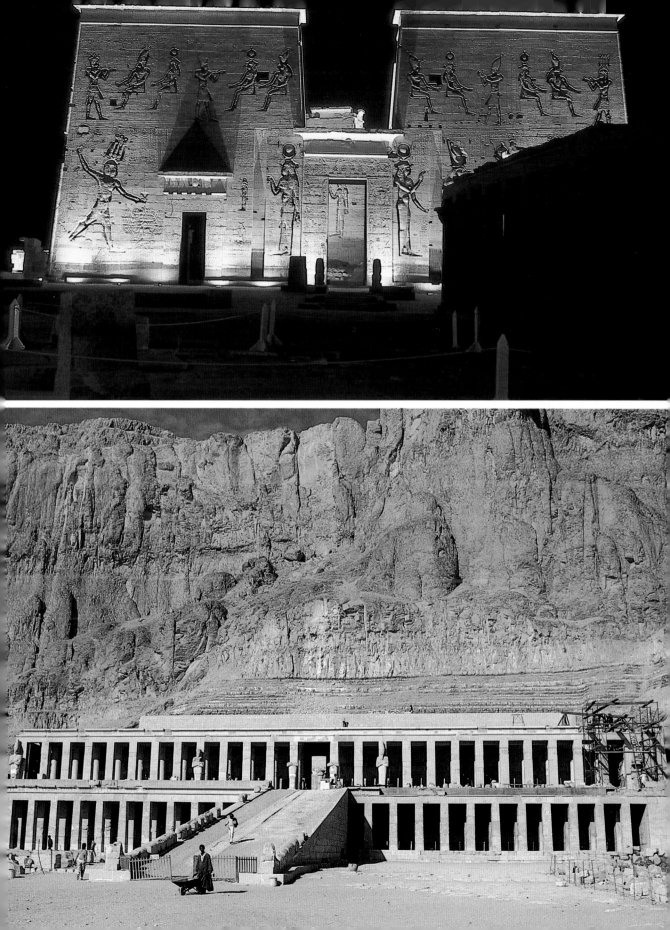

Not everyone could afford large, decorated tombs. But each person wanted to be buried in the best style that the family could afford. Ordinary citizens saved up all their lives for a proper death. Poorer classes buried their dead in simple graves with a few items of personal property.

Art with a Purpose

Egypt's pharaohs ordered gigantic building projects. They had a very practical purpose: to please the gods. And the more beautiful a structure was, the more pleased the gods would be.

We don't know the names of most of the people who built Egypt's monuments. Thousands of construction workers, stone cutters, sculptors, painters, and draftsmen did the labor. All worked for the gods under the direction of master architects and artists.

Egyptian art has a style all its own. For instance, people are shown with their chests facing forward and the rest of the body sideways. The more important a person was, the bigger the statue or painting. That explains why pyramids—the tombs of kings—were so large.

The Egyptian word for pyramid was *mr.* The Greeks named them *pyramids* after a kind of wheat cake with a similar shape. Kings of the First and Second Dynasties were buried in mastabas. These are tombs shaped like pyramids with their tops cut off. They were made of sun-dried mud-bricks. Stone was first used for building during the Third Dynasty.

The first true pyramid was built during the reign of Djoser, a Third Dynasty king. It was a step pyramid, built like several mastabas piled on top of each other. Its sides were like stair-steps. Later pyramids had an outer layer of granite or limestone, which gave them smooth sides.

In the Fourth Dynasty, millions of huge stone blocks were used to build the most famous pyramids, those at Giza. The stones were cut from nearby quarries and loaded onto barges on the Nile. At Giza, they were unloaded onto wooden sledges, or sliding carts. Workmen dragged the sledges to the building sites with ropes. Then they hauled the blocks into place, layer by layer, along crushed-stone ramps.

The pyramids look smaller now than they did in ancient times. Sand has built up around their bases, and the outer layer of blocks is gone. Most of these outer blocks were removed long ago and used for buildings in Cairo.

Under Amun's Shadow
Two great temples have survived from ancient Thebes: Karnak and Luxor. Karnak, where the god Amun was worshipped, was begun in the Middle Kingdom. Small at first, the original building became an enormous complex of unequalled beauty during Dynasties 18, 19, and 20. The top photo shows one of the entrances to the temple of Karnak. The temple of Luxor, much smaller, was also dedicated to Amun. The bottom photo shows the columns around the sun-court of Amun-hotep III, who began building the Luxor temple. Ramesses II (the Great) of the Nineteenth Dynasty finished it. The Luxor temple was the site of an important annual festival, called the Feast of Opet. At that time, statues of Amun, his wife the mother-goddess Mut, and their son the moon-god Khonsu were placed in sacred boats to travel to other towns along the Nile.

Timeline of Ancient Egyptian History

(All dates are approximate.)

About 5500 B.C.	**Earliest permanent human settlements in the Nile Valley**
3300–3100 B.C.	**Predynastic Period**
3150–3050 B.C.	Upper and Lower Egypt are unified. Narmer is one of the first kings.
3100–2750 B.C.	**Archaic or Early Dynastic Period** Dynasties 1 and 2
2750–2250 B.C.	**Old Kingdom or Pyramid Age** Dynasties 3–6 Memphis is Egypt's capital.
2650–2550 B.C.	Pyramids at Giza are built.
2250–2050 B.C.	**First Intermediate Period** Dynasties 7–10 and early Dynasty 11
2050–1650 B.C.	**Middle Kingdom** Reign of Neb-hepet-Ra Mentu-hotep II (Dynasty 11) and Dynasties 12–13 Thebes is made the capital.
2050 B.C.	Temple of Karnak is begun.
1720–1570 B.C.	**Second Intermediate Period** Dynasties 14–17
1570–1070 B.C.	**New Kingdom** Dynasties 18–20 Temple of Karnak is completed. Temple of Luxor is built.
1300 B.C.	Temples at Abu Simbel are carved.
1070–665 B.C.	**Third Intermediate Period** Dynasties 21–25 and early Dynasty 26
665–332 B.C.	**Late Period** Reign of Psammetichus I (Dynasty 26) and Dynasties 27–31
332–323 B.C.	**Alexander the Great**
323–30 B.C.	**Ptolemaic Period**
30 B.C.–A.D. 330	**Roman Period**

Writing in Hieroglyphs

To depict an object in hieroglyphs, the Egyptians just drew a picture of it. But to show ideas, they used homophones—words that sound alike but have different meanings. They added special symbols to show whether the word was a noun or verb, singular or plural, feminine or masculine. Thus, the sign for "house" could be used to write the similar-sounding word that meant "to go forth." Then the scribe would add a drawing of walking legs, the symbol for verbs of motion.

By about 300 B.C., there were over 400 hieroglyphs in use. But most common words could be written with fewer than fifty signs.

Knowledge of how to read hieroglyphs began to die out around the fourth century A.D. In 1799, French soldiers invading Egypt discovered the Rosetta Stone. On this slab, the same ancient decree was written in three scripts: hieroglyphs, *demotic*, and ancient Greek. By 1822, the French scholar Jean-Francois Champollion had found the clue for deciphering hieroglyphs by comparing the three.

Avenue of the Sphinxes

On the two previous pages is a view of the Avenue of the Sphinxes in the modern town of Luxor. Each sphinx has the head of a ram, a sacred animal of the god Amun. Archaeologists excavated the sphinxes and brought them together at the entrance to the temple of Karnak. The ancient processional avenue is now partly buried under the houses and shops of modern Luxor. It once led south from the temple of Karnak to the temple of Luxor. In this area, one can see centuries of Egyptian architecture. Nearly every great king of the Middle and New Kingdoms left some trace here.

Architectural Giants

(*Upper left*) The temple of Karnak' Hypostyle Hall. Pharaoh Sety I began its construction, and his son Ramesses II completed it in about 1250 B.C. The hall is 330 feet (100 meters) long and 160 feet (50 meters) wide. Within it is a "forest" of 122 sandstone pillars. (*Upper right* The Colossi of Memnon, at West Thebes. These seated giants, carved from quartzite, are almost all that remain of Pharaoh Amun-hotep III's memorial temple. (*Bottom*) The ruins of the temple of Khnum on the Island of Elephantine, near Aswan. Its granite blocks were brought from nearby quarries on large rollers that slid over the ground It is hard to imagine how such work were built with little more than simple tools.

Memphis, Capital of the Old Kingdom

Memphis was Egypt's capital during the Old Kingdom period—about 2750 B.C. to 2250 B.C. The city lay about 15 miles (25 kilometers) south of Cairo, Egypt's present-day capital. It was an important river port and must have been a splendid city. However, most of what we know about ancient Memphis comes from monuments in its cemeteries. These include the pyramids of Saqqara, Giza, and Dahshur.

At Saqqara is the step pyramid of King Djoser. It was designed by Imhotep, Djoser's vizier or prime minister. This is one of the few cases where we know the name of the architect. Imhotep was also famous as a physician and writer.

North of ancient Memphis, on the Giza Plateau, stand the three best known pyramids. They are the tombs of the Fourth Dynasty kings Khufu, Kha-ef-Ra, and Men-kau-Ra. (These kings are often called by their Greek names: Cheops, Chephren, and Mycerinus.) Built between 2650 and 2550 B.C., these pyramids are gigantic in size.

The pyramid of Khufu (Cheops) is the largest. It measures 480 feet (147 meters) high and 750 feet (230 meters) wide. Hemiun, Khufu's vizier, designed it. More than two million limestone blocks were used, some of them weighing over fifteen tons. According to the Greek historian Herodotus, over 100,000 men labored for twenty years to build it. They worked year round, even when the Nile overflowed its banks.

The pyramid of Kha-ef-Ra (Chephren) is slightly smaller than Khufu's. It looks taller because it stands on higher ground. The smallest of the three is the pyramid of Men-kau-Ra (Mycerinus).

Limestone blocks for these pyramids came from quarries on the Giza Plateau. The pyramids of Khufu and Kha-ef-Ra had outer layers of white limestone from the Tura quarries across the Nile. Men-kau-Ra's pyramid was cased in polished red granite from the quarries at Aswan. The stones were fitted together beautifully, especially in hallways and interior rooms. Inside the pyramids is a winding maze of passageways. To find the center and then get back out again was quite a task.

In front of the pyramid of Kha-ef-Ra is the Great Sphinx of Giza. It is the most famous sphinx in Egypt, and one of the oldest. All sphinxes have the body of a lion, the king of beasts. Some, like the Great Sphinx, have the head of the king, or pharaoh. Others have the head of a queen or a ram.

After the Fourth Dynasty, the Egyptian economy went into a slump. Kings could no longer afford such lavish building projects. Pyramids and statues of kings became smaller.

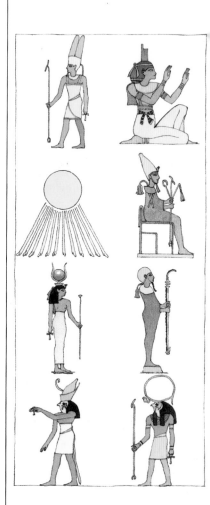

The Pyramids, Symbols of Egyptian Civilization

The top photo shows the most common image of ancient Egypt: the pyramids of Giza, located about five miles from modern Cairo. They were built between 2650 and 2550 B.C. The pyramid of King Khufu is the largest, followed by those of Kha-ef-Ra and Men-kau-Ra. The bottom photo shows a wall painting in a nobleman's tomb at Deir el-Medina in the necropolis of Thebes.

25

At Dahshur, another site in the Memphis area, are five pyramids of the Middle Kingdom period. Three of them are made of stone and two of sun-dried mud-bricks.

Thebes: Middle and New Kingdoms

Around 2250 B.C., Egypt broke apart into many separate nomes, or districts. About 2050 B.C., King Neb-hepet-Ra Mentu-hotep II unified the country once again. He made his capital at Thebes, on the bank of the Nile in Upper Egypt. This marks the beginning of the Middle Kingdom period.

About 1690 B.C., a people called the Hyksos took control of Egypt. They made the city of Avaris in the Nile Delta their capital. A century later, King Ahmose of the Eighteenth Dynasty drove the Hyksos out. This began the New Kingdom period. For much of this time, Thebes in the south and Memphis in the north shared the role of Egypt's capital.

The ruins of ancient Thebes are spread out over a large area. On the east bank of the Nile is the great temple of Karnak, dedicated to the god Amun. The temple was begun during the Middle Kingdom period. Pharaohs of the Eighteenth, Nineteenth, and Twentieth Dynasties added to it, making it the largest religious complex in the world.

The Karnak temple is filled with architectural marvels. Its monumental gateway is breathtaking. The great Hypostyle Hall is famous for its "forest" of gigantic decorated columns. And there are the granite obelisks—tall, pointy stone spires— that seem to point to heaven.

The Avenue of the Sphinxes, lined with rams-head sphinxes, led south from Karnak to the smaller temple of Luxor. This temple, too, was dedicated to the god Amun.

On the west bank of the Nile are the famous necropolises, or "cities of the dead"—the Valley of the Kings, the Valley of the Queens, and the Tombs of the Nobles. Pharaohs of the New Kingdom chose the Valley of the Kings as their final resting place. Royal ladies and a few princes were buried in the nearby Valley of the Queens.

Dotting the west bank are the remains of other monuments. There are the Colossi of Memnon, from the time of Amun-hotep III. At Deir el-Bahri is Queen Hat-shepsut's funerary temple, hewn out of rock. Then there is the great temple of Ramesses III at Medinet Habu. Its painted reliefs show battles between the Egyptians and the so-called Sea Peoples from Mediterranean lands to the north.

Monuments of Imperial Thebes
The top photo shows some of the columns surrounding the court of Ramesses II at the temple of Luxor. Gigantic statues of the king stand between the columns. Below is a close-up view of some of the ram-headed sphinxes at the temple of Karnak.

The Female Pharaoh

Egyptians believed their kings were living gods. Thus the mothers, wives, sisters, and daughters of kings played special roles. To keep royal blood "in the family," a pharaoh-to-be was expected to marry his sister or half-sister. If a king had no son, a non-royal man might marry the king's daughter or sister. Then their children would have royal (divine) blood. A few royal ladies even reigned as supreme ruler of Egypt themselves. Since kingship was a male role, ruling queens sometimes had to take on male clothing and titles. That was the case with the famous Hat-shepsut.

About 1504 B.C., King Tuthmosis II died. His widow and half-sister Hat-shepsut then ruled for her young stepson Tuthmosis III until he could grow up. However, this was not enough for Hat-shepsut. After all, she was the daughter of King Tuthmosis I. So she was a king's daughter, a king's sister, and a king's wife—the most royal lady in all of Egypt. Hat-shepsut had herself declared "king." Then she ruled jointly with her stepson as the senior partner on the throne.

"King" Hat-shepsut reigned for 22 years. During that time, she stamped out the last traces of foreign Hyksos rule. The country entered a period of peace, prosperity, and cultural development. In Egyptian art, Hat-shepsut was often portrayed wearing the clothing of a male ruler.

For a short time during the Eighteenth Dynasty, Egypt had a different capital city. Pharaoh Amun-hotep IV rejected Egypt's many traditional gods. Instead, he exalted just one god, a sun-god called the Aten. The king changed his name to Akh-en-Aten and founded a new capital, Akhet-Aten, known today as El-Amarna.

Akh-en-Aten's ideas completely changed the religion, politics, and arts of Egypt. The revolution was short-lived, though. After Tut-ankh-Amun ("King Tut") came to power, Akhet-Aten was abandoned and the government returned to Memphis and Thebes.

Magnificent Thebes

Thebes is best known for the temples of Karnak and Luxor. But there are many other sites in the area that are of great interest and beauty. The Ramesseum (*opposite page, top*) is the ruined funerary temple of Ramesses II. The photo below it shows a detail from the funerary temple of Ramesses III at Medinet Habu. A ceremonial palace was built against the south wall of this temple. In later times, the temple became a walled village and housed a Christian church.

The Great Pharaoh

Ramesses II ruled during the thirteenth century B.C. This huge statue (*left*) was erected in his honor in the temple of Luxor. As with other royal statues, it has the dignified pose and the colossal size that symbolize the pharaoh's power.

Nubia and Aswan

Nubia is an ancient region extending south from the city of Aswan. The pharaohs of Egypt occupied Nubia from time to time. And, for a brief period, Nubian kings ruled Egypt as the Twenty-fifth Dynasty. Many temples, tombs, and towns were left in Nubia from its days of glory.

In 1960, construction began on the Aswan High Dam. The dam was built to control the water of the Nile River and to produce hydroelectric power. But it would also create an artificial lake, Lake Nasser. The waters of this reservoir would cover the area's many artistic treasures, embodying centuries of history.

UNESCO sent out word of the danger, and 22 nations responded. An international team of engineers set to work. They took on the task of moving endangered monuments to higher ground. Precious temples were carefully cut into blocks and relocated, stone by stone, in new sites safely away from the water.

The laborious project was completed in 1972. Thus it is still possible today for us to enjoy such wonders as the temple of Ramesses II at Abu Simbel.

This temple was dedicated to the gods Amun, Ra, and Ptah and to the pharaoh Ramesses II. He ordered the temple to be carved around 1250 B.C. Its facade, 125 feet (38 meters) high, is decorated with four huge seated statues of Ramesses II, three of which are still well preserved. These are some of the largest ever created by ancient Egyptian sculptors. The rock-cut interior of the temple is also enormous—207 feet (63 meters) in depth.

The Temple of Hat-Hor, much smaller, was carved at Abu Simbel about the same time, also by command of Ramesses II. It was dedicated to the goddess Hat-Hor, represented by Queen Nefertari, Ramesses' favorite wife. Alternating statues of the pharaoh and his queen adorn the facade. The interior is similar in structure to the great temple at Abu Simbel.

We know of many more remains from ancient Nubia. Among them are the temples of Qertassi, Wadi es-Sebua, Derr, Buhen, Mirgissa, and Soleb. Some of these temples were saved from the waters, too. They have been moved to the outdoor archaeological park near the Aswan High Dam. Now, from high ground, they overlook the calm waters of Lake Nasser. Their natural surroundings may have changed with the passing of time, but the buildings still stand, faithful to centuries of history.

These Sites Are Part of the World Heritage

Memphis, its necropolis, and the pyramids at Giza and Dahshur. Memphis, capital of the Old Kingdom, is 15 miles (25 kilometers) from present-day Cairo. The oldest known pyramid, King Djoser's step pyramid, still stands in the area at Saqqara. On the Giza Plateau are the most famous pyramids—those of Khufu, Kha-ef-Ra, and Men-kau-Ra—and the Great Sphinx.

Thebes and its necropolis. Thebes was a capital of Egypt during the Middle and New Kingdoms. In the area of Thebes are the splendid temples of Karnak and Luxor and the famous necropolises, or cities of the dead—the Valley of the Kings, the Valley of the Queens, and the Tombs of the Nobles.

The monuments of Nubia and Aswan were moved to higher ground to save them from the waters of Lake Nasser. The most famous of them all are the temples of Ramesses II and Queen Nefertari at Abu Simbel.

Glossary

afterlife: life after death

archaeologist: a scientist who learns about the past by studying the remains of ancient objects and buildings

barge: a flat-bottomed boat for transporting heavy loads on a river

colossus: (plural, colossi) a gigantic statue

decipher: to figure out the meaning of something hidden or unclear

delta: the fertile area around the branching mouth of a river; named after a triangle-shaped letter of the Greek alphabet

demotic: an ancient form of writing derived from hieroglyphics

dynasty: a family of rulers who pass their leadership down to family members

excavate: to dig up out of the ground

facade: the front or face of a building, often having a special design or extra decoration

funerary: having to do with a burial

hieroglyphic: ancient Egyptian form of writing using simple pictures as characters (each character is a hieroglyph)

internist: a doctor of general medicine, as opposed to a surgeon or a specialist for one part of the body

kiosk: a small building with open sides

mastaba: a one-story tomb structure with sloping sides; used as kings' tombs during Egypt's First and Second Dynasties

monsoons: fierce winds and rainstorms occurring every year in southern Asia and the Indian Ocean area

mortuary chapel: a room where funerals are held and prayers for the dead are offered

mummy: a body prepared for burial by drying and treatment with preservatives to prevent decay

necropolis: literally, "city of the dead"; a cemetery

obelisk: a tall, four-sided stone pillar that narrows at the top to a pyramid-like point

papyrus: a tall plant of the Nile Valley; the spongy tissue in its stem can be pressed into a kind of writing paper

pharaoh: a title for kings of Egypt after about 1500 B.C.; from the word *per-aa*, meaning the king's house

pyramid: a structure with triangular sides and usually a square base; ancient Egyptian tombs were built in this shape

quarry: an open pit dug to obtain stone for building

relief: a sculpture that stands out from the wall or other flat surface on which it is carved

scroll: a roll of writing material on which a document is written

sphinx: a statue with the body of a lion and the head of an animal or a person

step pyramid: a tomb with sides like stair-steps

vizier: a prime minister or other high court officer

Index

Page numbers in boldface type indicate illustrations.

Abu Simbel, 6, **7, 8–9,** 30, **31**
Ahmose, 26
Akh-en-Aten, 28
Amun (god), 6, 18, 22, 26, 30
Amun-hotep III, 18, 22, 26
Amun-hotep IV, 28
art, unique style of, 16, 18
astronomy, 14
Aswan, 6, 30, **31**
Aswan High Dam, 4, 8, **12,** 30
Aten (god), 6, 28
Avaris, 26
Avenue of the Sphinxes, **20–21,** 22, 26
Book of the Dead, 16
Buhen, 30
Cairo, 10, 18, 24
Carnarvon, Lord, 14
Carter, Howard, 14
Champollion, Jean-Francois, 22
Colossi of Memnon, 22, **23,** 26
construction methods, 18, 22, 24
Dahshur, 24, 26, 31
dead, treatment of, 4, 12, 14, 16, 18
Deir el-Bahri, 16, **17,** 26
Deir el-Medina, 24, **25**
Derr, 30
Djoser, 14, 18, 24
doctors and prescriptions, 14
economy of ancient Egypt, 6, 10, 24
Egyptian Antiquities Organization, 12
Egyptian Museum, 14
El-Amarna (Akhet-Aten), 28
Elephantine, Island of, 22, **23**
farming, 6, 10
Feast of Opet, 18
food, 10
Giza, pyramids of, 4, **5,** 10, 18, 24, **25, 31**
gods and goddesses, 6, 18, 28
Hat-Hor (goddess), 6, 8, 30, **31**
Hat-shepsut, 16, 26
Hemiun, 24
Herodotus, 24
hieroglyphic writing, 14, 22
history of Egypt, 6, 12, 14, 22, 24, 26, 28
Horus (god), 6
Hyksos, 26
Hypostyle Hall, 22, **23,** 26
Imhotep, 24
Isis (goddess), 6
ka (soul), 16
Karnak, temple of, 18, **19,** 22, 26, **27, 31**
Kha-ef-Ra (Chephren), 10, 24
Khnum, temple of, 22, **23**
Khufu (Cheops), 4, 24
kings as gods, 6, 12, 14, 26
life after death, belief in, 14, 16
Luxor (town), 12, 14, 22

Luxor, temple of, 18, **19,** 22, 26, **27, 28**
Mandulis, temple of, **16**
map of ancient Egypt, **10**
mastabas, 4, 14, **15,** 18
mathematics, 14
Medinet Habu, 26, **29**
Mediterranean Sea, 6, 26
Memphis, 10, **11,** 24, 26, 28, **31**
Men (Menes), 12
Men-kau-Ra (Mycerinus), 24
Middle Kingdom period, 18, 22, 26
Mirgissa, 30
mummies, 14, 16
Nasser, Lake, 8, 30
Neb-hepet-Ra Mentu-hotep II, 26
Nefertari, 8, 30, **31**
New Kingdom period, 22, 26
Nile Delta, 4, 6, 12, 26
Nile River, 4, 6, 14, 18, 24, 26, 30
Nubia, 12, 30
Old Kingdom period, 24
Opening of the Mouth, 16
Osiris (god), 6, 16
papyrus, 10, 14, 16
"pharaoh," origin of word, 12
Philae, temple of, 16, **17**
Ptah (god), 6, 30
pyramids, 4, **5, 15,** 18, 24, **25,** 26
Qertassi, Kiosk of, **12,** 30
Ra (god), 6, 14, 30
Ramesses I, 12, **13**
Ramesses II, 6, **7, 8–9,** 18, 22, 26, **27, 28, 29,** 30, **31**
Ramesses III, 12, **13,** 26, **29**
religion, 14, 16, 28
Rosetta Stone, 22
Saqqara, 14, 24
Sea Peoples, 26
Sety I, 22
social classes, 12
Soleb, 30
Sphinx of Giza (Great Sphinx), 10, 24, **31**
sphinxes, 10, **11, 20–21,** 22, 24, **27, 31**
step pyramids, 14, **15,** 18, 24
temples, 4, 6, **7,** 8, **8–9, 12, 13,** 14, 16, **17,** 18, **19,** 26, **27, 28, 29,** 30
Thebes, 4, 12, **13,** 16, **17,** 24, **25,** 26, 28, **31**
tombs, **5,** 12, **13,** 14, 16, 18
Tombs of the Nobles, 12, 26
Tut-ankh-Amun, 4, **5,** 14, 28
Tuthmosis I, II, and III, 26
UNESCO, 8, 30, 35
Valley of the Kings, 4, 12, 14, 26
Valley of the Queens, 12, 26
Wadi es-Sebua, 30
Weighing of the Heart, 16
World Heritage sites, 30, 31, 35

Titles in the World Heritage Series

The Land of the Pharaohs
The Chinese Empire
Ancient Greece
Prehistoric Rock Art
The Roman Empire
Mayan Civilization
Tropical Rain Forests
Inca Civilization
Prehistoric Stone Monuments
Romanesque Art and Architecture
Great Animal Refuges of the World
Coral Reefs

Photo Credits

All the photographs in this volume were taken by
Michel Escobar and Veronique Hemery/Incafo.

Project Editor, Childrens Press: Ann Heinrichs
Original Text: Marinella Terzi
Subject Consultant: Dr. John Larson
Translator: Angela Ruiz
Design: Alberto Caffaratto
Cartography: Modesto Arregui
Drawings: Federico Delicado
Phototypesetting: Publishers Typesetters, Inc.

UNESCO's World Heritage

The United Nations Educational, Scientific, and Cultural Organization (UNESCO) was founded in 1946. Its purpose is to contribute to world peace by promoting cooperation among nations through education, science, and culture. UNESCO believes that such cooperation leads to universal respect for justice, for the rule of law, and for the basic human rights of all people.

UNESCO's many activities include, for example, combatting illiteracy, developing water resources, educating people on the environment, and promoting human rights.

In 1972, UNESCO established its World Heritage Convention. With members from over 100 nations, this international body works to protect cultural and natural wonders throughout the world. These include significant monuments, archaeological sites, geological formations, and natural landscapes. Such treasures, the Convention believes, are part of a World Heritage that belongs to all people. Thus, their preservation is important to us all.

Specialists on the World Heritage Committee have targeted over 300 sites for preservation. Through technical and financial aid, the international community restores, protects, and preserves these sites for future generations.

Volumes in the *World Heritage* series feature spectacular color photographs of various World Heritage sites and explain their historical, cultural, and scientific importance.